Unusual Pets

MARYSA STORM

BOLT

Bolt is published by Black Rabbit Books
P.O. Box 227, Mankato, Minnesota, 56002.
www.blackrabbitbooks.com

Alissa Thielges, editor; Rhea Magaro, designer and photo researcher

Library of Congress Cataloging-in-Publication Data
Names: Storm, Marysa, author.
Title: Tarantulas / by Marysa Storm.
Description: Mankato, MN: Bolt is published by Black Rabbit Books, [2026] | Series: Unusual pets | Includes bibliographical references and index. | Audience: Ages 8-12 | Audience: Grades 4-6
Identifiers: LCCN 2024043413 (print) | LCCN 2024043414 (ebook) | ISBN 9781644667835 (library binding) | ISBN 9781644667958 (ebook)
Subjects: LCSH: Tarantulas—Juvenile literature.
Classification: LCC QL458.42.T5 S884 2026 (print) | LCC QL458.42.T5 (ebook) | DDC 595.4/4—dc23/eng/20241220
LC record available at https://lccn.loc.gov/2024043413

Image Credits

Alamy Stock Photo/imageBROKER/C. Steimer, 21 (bottom), Juniors Bildarchiv / F314, 21 (top); Dreamstime/Werg, 24 (bottom); Shutterstock/Aastels, 4–5, Antonio Gravante, 22, asawinimages, 32, Audrey Snider-Bell, 6, Benny Marty, 15, Bruno_Leslle, 3, Cornel Constantin, 16, DAL Photography, 1, Eillen, 23, Green Wall Std, 11, Lapis2380, 22, Le Rygal, 12–13, Macrovector, 26, MH Capture, 24 (top), mineral vision, 24 (middle), Nynke van Holten, 31, Photohobbiest, 23, Pixel-Shot, 8–9, 23, RMMPPhotography, cover, SEAN D THOMAS, 25, Spidergeek, 22–23, Tobias Hauke, 28–29, Uzo Borewicz, 27, Zoltan Mucsi, 18–19

CONTENTS

CHAPTER 1

Meet the

A young boy gazes into a tank. Inside is a huge spider. It is a tarantula! The boy gives his pet a wave. Wait…is that *another* one? The boy looks closer. He spots what looks like a second spider. Is it lying on its back? Nope! It is just his spider's old **exoskeleton**!

Alone Time

The boy was going to feed his spider, but not anymore. His spider just **molted**. He knows it needs to be left alone now. The boy checks the tank. It needs to be warm and **humid**. Then he backs away. His pet's new skin needs time to harden. Until it does, the spider could be easily hurt.

CHAPTER 2

A SPECIAL PET

Spiders are different than most pets. Instead of four legs, they have eight. They don't need to go on walks. And they aren't the best cuddlers. Most tarantulas are gentle. Some will walk across a person's body. But it is best if they are left alone. Owners can look, but they shouldn't often touch.

Tarantulas are most active at night.

WHERE TARANTULAS LIVE IN THE WILD

NORTH AMERICA

SOUTH AMERICA

EUROPE
ASIA
AFRICA
AUSTRALIA
ANTARCTICA

Taking One Home

In the wild, some tarantulas are **endangered**. People have taken too many to sell as pets. People should never take tarantulas from the wild. They need to be careful when buying them too. It is important to buy from a trustworthy place. **Breeders** know a lot about tarantulas and how to care for them.

Signs of a Good Breeder

- Knows the age
- Knows the sex (male or female)
- Knows the species
- Knows who the parents are

CHAPTER 3

Tarantula

There are about 900 species of tarantulas. Many pet tarantulas are Chilean rose or Mexican red-knee tarantulas. They are easier to care for.

COMPARING LENGTHS

Chilean rose tarantula

Mexican red-knee tarantula

Mexican redleg tarantula

length in inches

Tarantulas can live a long time. Males live to about 10 years old. Some females can live to 30! Some tarantulas are fully grown by age three. Others take 12 years to reach full size. Young tarantulas molt often as they grow.

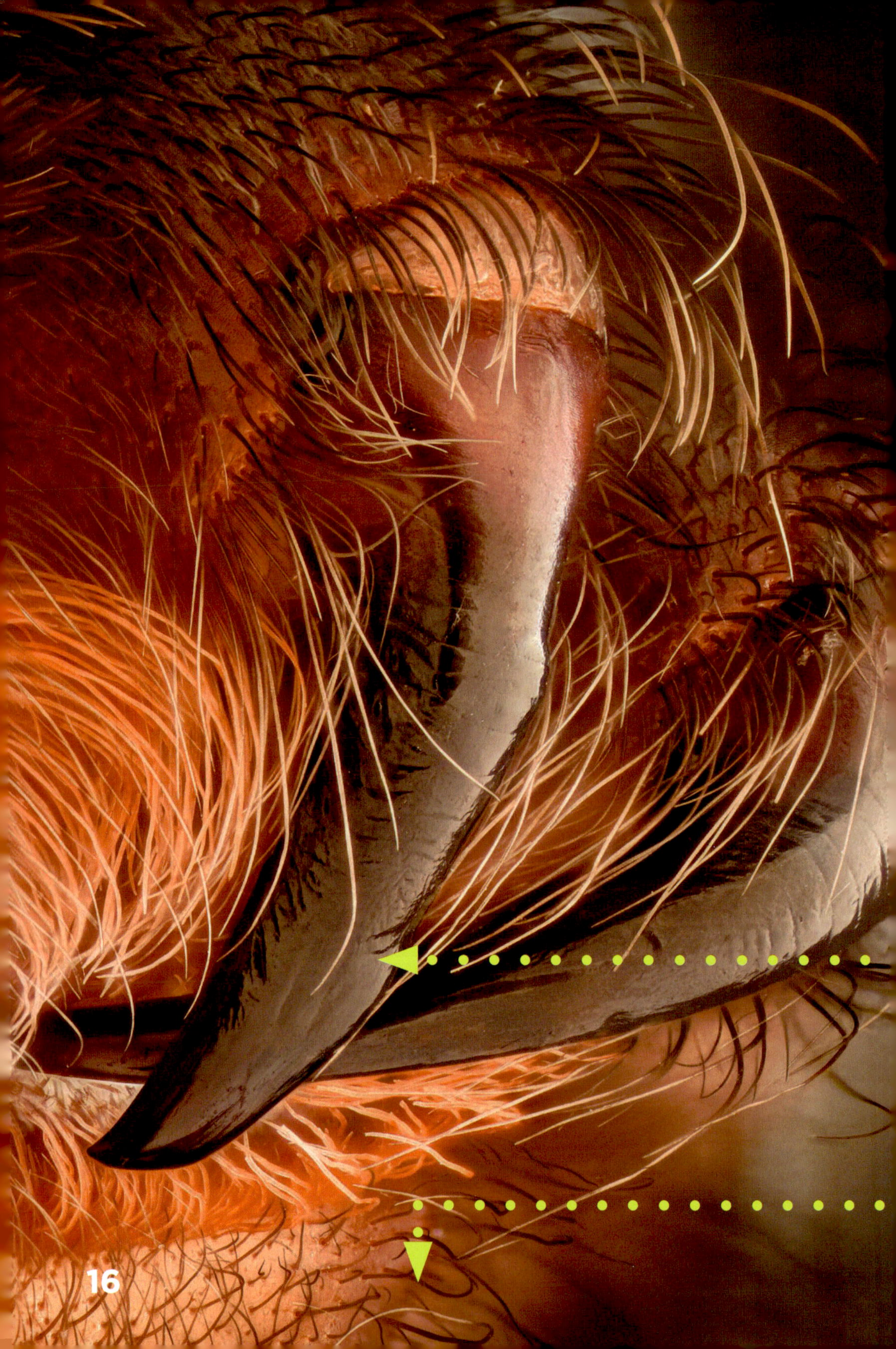

Fuzz and Fangs

All tarantulas are covered in short hairs. Some hairs are barbed. If startled, the pet can release them. The hairs attach to someone's skin and cause itching. These pets also have fangs and **venomous** bites. The venoms kills small prey that they eat. The bite won't kill a person. But it hurts!

about 0.03 inches (0.8 millimeters) long

PARTS OF A TARANTULA

EYES
LEGS
CLAWS

CHAPTER 4

Caring for a

Pet spiders are kept in big **terrariums**. A tight-fitting lid is key. Tarantulas are great climbers and like to escape.

Some tarantulas spend most of their time on the ground. Other types prefer to be in trees. Those spiders need taller tanks. They also need branches to climb and spin webs in. All tarantulas need places to hide.

Types of Terrariums

Ground tarantulas

Tree tarantulas

A TARANTULA TERRARIUM

place to hide

fake tree bark and plants

WHAT DO TARANTULAS EAT?

crickets

mealworms

superworms

Food and Water

Tarantulas are predators. It's important for them to be fed live insects. Crickets and mealworms are good choices. Big tarantulas can be given small mice and lizards. Most people feed their tarantulas once or twice a week. The tank should have a **shallow** dish of fresh water. If the dish is too deep, the spider could drown.

roaches

Special Care

Taking care of a tarantula means giving it space. They need a quiet place away from sunlight. Their tank should be kept warm. It's important to learn all about tarantulas before bringing one home. This will help give the spiders a good home.

The Right Temperature

70 to 80 degrees Fahrenheit (21 to 26.7 degrees Celsius)

40 to 90 percent humidity

0 10 20 30 40 50 60 70 80 90 100

By the NUMBERS

up to **12** inches (30 cm)

LENGTH OF THE LARGEST TARANTULA (GOLIATH BIRD-EATING TARANTULA)

15 minutes to **12** hours

TIME IT TAKES TO MOLT

8

NUMBER OF EYES

up to **1,000**

HOW MANY EGGS A FEMALE CAN LAY AT ONCE

GLOSSARY

breeder (BREE-der)—a person who raises animals with specific characteristics

endangered (en-DAYN-jurd)—close to no longer existing

exoskeleton (ek-so-SKE-le-ten)—the hard, protective cover on the outside of an insect's or arachnid's body

humid (hyoo-MID)—having a lot of moisture in the air

molt (MOLT)—to lose a covering of hair, feathers, or skin and replace it with new growth

shallow (SHAL-oh)—having a small distance to the bottom from the surface or highest point

terrarium (tuh-RAIR-ee-uhm)—a glass or plastic box that is used for growing plants or keeping small animals indoors

venomous (VEN-uh-mus)—containing venom or poison

BOOKS

Bow, James. *Tarantulas.* Mendota Heights, MN: Apex Editions, 2024.

Humphrey, Natalie. *Goliath Bird-Eating Spiders.* Buffalo, NY: Gareth Stevens Publishing, 2025.

Mallory, Louis. *Do You Want a Pet Tarantula?* Buffalo, NY: Enslow Publishing, 2025.

WEBSITES

Animals: Tarantulas
www.ducksters.com/animals/tarantula.php

Tarantula
kids.nationalgeographic.com/animals/invertebrates/facts/tarantula

Tarantula – Kids
kids.britannica.com/kids/article/tarantula/353837

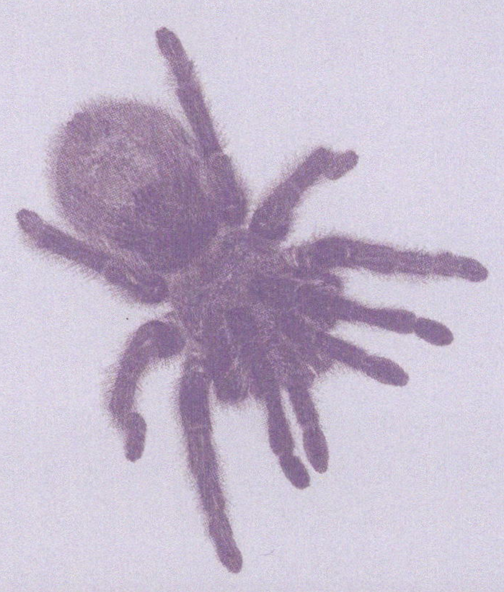

INDEX